P9-CAG-625

With love and appreciation
to Toni Von Hollen,
Creative Storyteller Extraordinaire,
her husband Richard,
and daughter Marissa.

THE REAL TWELVE DAYS OF CHRISTMAS

published by Multnomah Publishers, Inc.

©1997 by Helen Haidle

Illustrations © 1997 by Celeste Henriquez

International Standard Book Number: 1-57673-201-0

Scripture quotations taken from *The Holy Bible, New International Version*

©1973, 1984 by International Bible Society,

used by permission of Zondervan Publishing House

Printed in the United States of America

For information:

MULTNOMAH PUBLISHERS, INC.

POST OFFICE BOX 1720

SISTERS, OREGON 97759

99 00 01 02 03 04 05 — 10 9 8 7 6 5 4 3

THE REAL 12 DAYS OF CHRISTMAS

HELEN HAIDLE

illustrated by

CELESTE HENRIQUEZ

MULTNOMAH PUBLISHERS, SISTERS, OREGON

On the first day of Christmas, my true love gave to me a partridge in a pear tree.

On the second day of Christmas, my true love gave to me two turtledoves.

On the third day of Christmas, my true love gave to me three French hens.

On the fourth day of Christmas, my true love gave to me four calling birds.

On the fifth day of Christmas, my true love gave to me five golden rings.

On the sixth day of Christmas, my true love gave to me six geese a-laying.

On the seventh day of Christmas, my true love gave to me seven swans a-swimming.

On the eighth day of Christmas, my true love gave to me eight maids a-milking.

On the ninth day of Christmas, my true love gave to me nine ladies dancing.

On the tenth day of Christmas, my true love gave to me ten lords a-leaping.

On the eleventh day of Christmas, my true love gave to me eleven pipers piping.

On the twelfth day of Christmas, my true love gave to me twelve drummers drumming.

Foreword

Do French hens, gold rings, and milking maids have anything to do with the Christian faith? Is it possible that a fun and rollicking Christmas carol might have a deeper, hidden message? What is the real meaning behind "The Twelve Days of Christmas?" In the sixteenth century, England proclaimed an official state church, and any other religious teaching was strictly forbidden. So for the next three centuries, those who refused to join the state church developed creative ways to teach children their beliefs. One popular method was to use lyrics and song. On the following pages, you will discover the secret Christian symbols concealed in the familiar carol, "The Twelve Days of Christmas." This cheerful song, about a generous benefactor who loved to give, could be freely sung without ever using God's name, because "my true love" refers to God. So come along and discover for yourself how things are not always as they seem. See how an old familiar carol overflows with rich spiritual significance. And the next time you sing this song, notice how even the repetitive pattern represents a special meaning – as the verses repeat over and over, so God's ongoing gifts and blessings continue to flow.

Every good and perfect gift is from above,
coming down from the Father of the heavenly lights,
who does not change like shifting shadows.
He chose to give us birth through the word of truth.

JAMES 1:17-18

The FIRST DAY

On the first day of Christmas, my true love gave to me a partridge in a pear tree. The first gift of this Christmas song is a partridge, a small bird similar to a quail or a grouse. The original gift of Christmas is Jesus, sent to earth from God. "For God so loved the world that he gave his one and only Son." JOHN 3:16 The partridge was known as a valiant bird, willing to fight to the death in order to defend its young. This bird's readiness to die for its young made it an ancient Christian symbol of Christ. The pear tree represents the cross.

I am the good shepherd....I lay down my life for the sheep.
JOHN 10:14-15

The
SECOND DAY

On the second day of Christmas, my true love gave to me two turtledoves. For hundreds of years, Jewish families used turtledoves as offerings to God. The gift of two turtledoves is a reminder of the sacrifice offered for Jesus by Mary and Joseph. When Jesus was forty days old, they took him to the temple in Jerusalem. They brought a sacrifice of two turtledoves as was required by the law.

Joseph and Mary took him to Jerusalem to present him to the Lord...and to offer a sacrifice in keeping with what is said in the Law of the Lord: "a pair of doves or two young pigeons."

LUKE 2:22, 24

The THIRD DAY

On the third day of Christmas, my true love gave to me three French hens. French hens were valuable poultry during the sixteenth century – only the rich could afford them. These costly birds symbolized the three valuable gifts given to Jesus by the wise men: gold, frankincense, and myrrh. Gold was the most precious of all metals. Frankincense and myrrh were expensive spices used as incense and for burials.

When they [wise men] saw the star, they were
overjoyed. On coming to the house, they saw the child...and they bowed
down and worshiped him. Then they opened their treasures and presented
him with gifts of gold and of incense and of myrrh.

MATTHEW 2:10-11

The
FOURTH DAY

On the fourth day of Christmas, my true love gave to me four calling birds. The four calling birds are reminders of the four Gospel writers: Matthew, Mark, Luke, and John. These writers of the first four books of the New Testament proclaimed the testimony of Jesus' life and teachings. Like birds calling out with loud and distinctive voices, Matthew, Mark, Luke, and John spread abroad the news of Jesus' life, death, and resurrection. They called people to faith in Jesus as their Savior.

Jesus did many other miraculous signs...which are not recorded in this book. But these are written that you may believe that Jesus is the Christ, the Son of God, and that by believing you may have life in his name.

JOHN 20:30-31

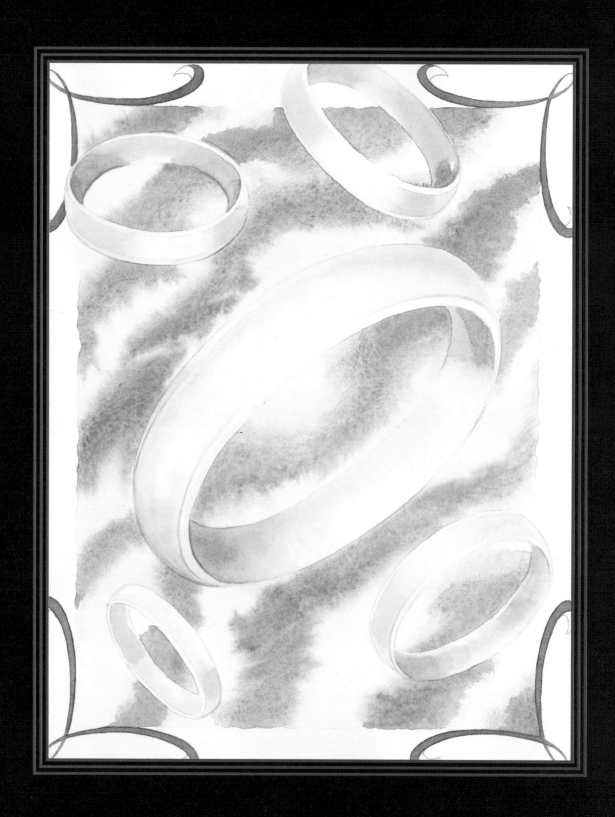

The FIFTH DAY

On the fifth day of Christmas, my true love gave to me five golden rings. Gold rings are among the most valuable and treasured of all gifts. The five golden rings represent the first five books of the Old Testament: Genesis, Exodus, Leviticus, Numbers, and Deuteronomy. These books, known to the Jews as the Torah, were treated with great reverence and considered to be worth more than gold. In these books, Moses, the commonly accepted author, records the creation story and the beginning history of the people of Israel.

No prophet has risen in Israel like Moses, whom the Lord knew face to face....for no one has ever shown the mighty power or performed the awesome deeds that Moses did in the sight of all Israel.

DEUTERONOMY 34:10, 12

The SIXTH DAY

On the sixth day of Christmas, my true love gave to me six geese a-laying. In many cultures, eggs symbolize new life. Six geese laying eggs become reminders of the six days of creation when God, by his Word, brought forth life on earth. God spoke and filled the earth with plants, birds, animals, and people during the first six days of creation, as found in chapter one of the book of Genesis.

In the beginning God created the heavens and the earth....
God saw all that he had made, and it was very good. And there was evening,
and there was morning — the sixth day.

GENESIS 1:1, 31

The
SEVENTH DAY

On the seventh day of Christmas, my true love gave to me seven swans a-swimming. Seven swans symbolize the seven gifts of the Holy Spirit. Just as baby swans grow and change from "ugly ducklings" into beautiful and graceful birds, so do God's children grow and change through the work of the Holy Spirit. The various gifts of the Holy Spirit are distributed for the benefit of the entire body of Christ.

We have different gifts, according to the grace given us.
If a man's gift is prophesying, let him use it in proportion to his faith.
If it is serving, let him serve; if it is teaching, let him teach;
if it is encouraging, let him encourage; if it is contributing to the needs
of others, let him give generously; if it is leadership, let him govern
diligently; if it is showing mercy, let him do it cheerfully.

ROMANS 12:6-8

The EIGHTH DAY

On the eighth day of Christmas, my true love gave to me eight maids a-milking. The eight milking maidens represent eight unique teachings of Jesus sometimes called the Beatitudes. These words of Jesus, from his Sermon on the Mount, nurture and strengthen us much the way milk nourishes a child.

Blessed are the poor in spirit....
Blessed are those who mourn....Blessed are the meek....
Blessed are those who hunger and thirst for righteousness....
Blessed are the merciful....Blessed are the pure in heart....
Blessed are the peacemakers....Blessed are those who
are persecuted because of righteousness.

MATTHEW 5:3-12

The
NINTH DAY

On the ninth day of Christmas, my true love gave to me nine ladies dancing. The nine ladies remind us of the nine different fruits that the Holy Spirit produces in the lives of God's children. ✒ Just as these ladies dance joyfully, so can every Christian rejoice over the life-changing fruit of the Holy Spirit. ✒ Gifts like love and joy and peace are worthy of great celebration!

*But the fruit of the Spirit is love, joy, peace, patience,
kindness, goodness, faithfulness, gentleness and self-control.*
GALATIANS 5:22-23

The TENTH DAY

On the tenth day of Christmas, my true love gave to me ten lords a-leaping. Lords were men with authority to command people's obedience. Ten lords a-leaping symbolize God's ten basic laws, otherwise known as the Ten Commandments.

You shall have no other gods. You shall not make and bow to any carved images. You shall not take the name of the Lord your God in vain. Remember the Sabbath day to keep it holy. Honor your father and your mother. You shall not murder. You shall not commit adultery. You shall not steal. You shall not bear false witness against your neighbor. You shall not covet your neighbor's things.

EXODUS 20:3-17 (PARAPHRASE)

The ELEVENTH DAY

On the eleventh day of Christmas, my true love gave to me eleven pipers piping. Eleven pipers represent the eleven apostles who were chosen by Jesus and remained faithful to him. (There were twelve before the betrayal and suicide of Judas.) Like children joyfully following a piper, these disciples followed Jesus. They also called others to follow him. They piped an everlasting tune of great joy – the salvation message of Jesus' resurrection from the dead.

These are the twelve [Jesus] appointed: Simon (to whom he gave the name Peter); James son of Zebedee and his brother John...Andrew, Philip, Bartholomew, Matthew, Thomas, James son of Alphaeus, Thaddaeus, Simon the Zealot and Judas Iscariot, who betrayed him.

MARK 3:16-19

The
TWELFTH DAY

On the twelfth day of Christmas, my true love gave to me twelve drummers drumming. Just as drummers beat out a loud, steady rhythm for marchers to follow, so the Apostle's Creed sets forth the beliefs of those who call themselves Christians. The twelve drummers represent the twelve vital Christian beliefs as stated in the Apostle's Creed.

I believe in God the Father Almighty, maker of heaven and earth.
I believe in Jesus Christ, his only Son, our Lord,
who was conceived by the Holy Spirit and born of the Virgin Mary.
He suffered under Pontius Pilate, was crucified, died, and was buried.
He descended into hell; the third day he rose from the dead.
He ascended into heaven and sits at the right hand of God the Father.
He shall return to judge both the living and the dead.
I believe in the Holy Spirit, the holy Christian church,
the communion of saints, the forgiveness of sins,
the resurrection of the body, and the life everlasting.

A Historical Look at Christmas Celebrations and Traditions

Around A.D. 350, December 25 was proclaimed as the date to commemorate Jesus' birth. ✒ January 6, called the Feast of the Epiphany, was celebrated as the day of the presentation of the Christ child to the wise men upon their arrival in Bethlehem. Epiphany reminds us that Jesus is the Savior for all humankind, not exclusively for the Jews. ✒ The first mention of the twelve days of Christmas dates back to the fourth century. In 567, the Council of Tours declared the twelve days between Christmas and Epiphany to be a festive period. The Feast of St. Stephen (December 26) and the Feast of St. John (December 27), plus a variety of Christmas and New Year customs and gift-giving activities filled those days. ✒ People ended the twelve days with festivities on the night of January 5 or January 6, depending on when the counting began. In England, December 26 was the first day. In Germany, Belgium, and Holland, the twelve days began on December 25.

CELEBRATING THE 12 DAYS OF CHRISTMAS

There are many ways to celebrate Christ's birth. You could begin on December 12 and celebrate the twelve days leading up to Christmas Day. This is also a good time to select activities to encourage others who are struggling through the holidays and need a special touch of love.

KEEP ON GIVING

Some families spread out the Christmas gift-giving during the twelve days after Christmas. Inexpensive after-Christmas sales can help extend your celebration. Children delight in opening a small gift each day.

SECRET GIVERS

Read together Matthew 6:1-4 and consider selecting a family, teacher, or neighbor as the recipient of secret giving during the twelve days before (or after) Christmas Day. Like in the song, "The Twelve Days of Christmas," you can find a corresponding number of creative gifts to give on each day. (For example: one small manger scene on the first day, two Christmas ornaments on the second day, ten cookies on the tenth day, etc.) On the twelfth day, write a simple card telling the recipient about Christ's love and that they are loved and being prayed for, and keep it anonymous, as Jesus suggested.

In the weeks before Christmas, set up a nativity scene in a prominent place. Position figures of the wise men and camels a distance away from the manger. As you approach Epiphany, January 6, move the figures closer to the manger, with arrival on Epiphany.

PLAN AN EPIPHANY PARTY

- Set up lots of candles, strings of small white lights, and star decorations.
- Bake a yellow "Epiphany cake" (add a large pitted date, dried fruit, or large gumdrop to batter).
- Read the story of the wise men in Matthew 2.
- Whoever finds the treat in their piece of cake gets to be king or queen of the party (they can preside over the festivities and lead in the games).
- Use a gold foil crown and a robe for the king or queen.
- Divide into small groups and let each group decide on a Bible story they will act out.
- Take turns pantomiming the stories while onlookers try to guess the stories.
- Take turns drawing Bible stories on a blackboard while others guess.

FINAL NOTE

Other spiritual doctrine that may have been symbolized in "The Twelve Days of Christmas":

- two testaments of the Bible
- three persons of the Trinity
- three gifts of faith, hope and love
- six days of the week that humanity labors
- eight people saved in Noah's ark
- nine ranks of angels
- twelve gates of heaven
- twelve tribes of Israel

Resource materials were found in the *1995 Sourcebook for Sundays and Seasons*, ©1994, Lawrence E. Mick (principal author and compiler), Archdiocese of Chicago: Liturgy Training Publications.

On the first day of Christmas, my true love gave to me a partridge in a pear tree.

On the second day of Christmas, my true love gave to me two turtledoves.

On the third day of Christmas, my true love gave to me three French hens.

On the fourth day of Christmas, my true love gave to me four calling birds.

On the fifth day of Christmas, my true love gave to me five golden rings.

On the sixth day of Christmas, my true love gave to me six geese a-laying.

On the seventh day of Christmas, my true love gave to me seven swans a-swimming.

On the eighth day of Christmas, my true love gave to me eight maids a-milking.

On the ninth day of Christmas, my true love gave to me nine ladies dancing.

On the tenth day of Christmas, my true love gave to me ten lords a-leaping.

On the eleventh day of Christmas, my true love gave to me eleven pipers piping.

On the twelfth day of Christmas, my true love gave to me twelve drummers drumming.